Arabellafella's First Reading Book

By Tagore Ramoutar

I like white flowers.

A daisy.

I like dollies.

A pile of dollies.

I like carrots.

Three carrots.

I like yellow flowers.

A buttercup.

I like jigsaws.

A jigsaw.

I like small cakes.

Cakes.

I like red flowers.

Red roses.

I really like drawing pictures.

Felt tip pens.

I really like strawberries!

Strawberries.

I really like pale pink flowers.

A wild rose.

I really like milk.

A glass of milk.

I really like books.

Books.

I love bananas.

A banana.

I love cuddly toys.

Cuddly toys.

I love birthday cakes.

A monkey cake.

I really love pink and purple flowers.

Fuchsias, my favourite!

First Published 2013.
Published under the brand name Eric and Rufus Children's Books, a brand of Longshot Ventures Ltd, UK. Copyright Tagore Ramoutar, Longshot Ventures Ltd.

Printed in the UK: ISBN 978-1-907837-52-4.
Printed by Amazon in US/UK/ Germany: ISBN 978-1-907837-79-1

www.ericandrufus.com